Tree standing small

Helen Allison

To Tes & Sandra,
Thank you & hope you
enjoy the book.

xx

CLOCH⊙DERICK

Tree standing small was first published in 2018
by Clochoderick Press.
First Edition.
www.clochoderickpress.co.uk

Twitter @h_allison_poet

Clochoderick Press
27 Newton Street, Paisley, Renfrewshire, Scotland, PA1 2RN

A CIP catalogue record for this book is available from the British Library.
ISBN: 978-1-912345-03-8

Typeset by R.K. Wallace in Dante

Printed and bound by:
Imprint Academic
Seychelles Farm, Upton Pyne, Exeter, Devon EX5 5HY

Funded by:

Photo by Ian Macrae

About Helen Allison

Helen lives in her native town of Forres, in the
north of Scotland. She has previously studied
English Language and Literature at Glasgow Uni-
versity. Her work has featured in a variety of re-
spected journals all over the country, with some
finishing in prominent positions in various literature competitions. *Tree standing small* is her first
published collection of poetry.

Acknowledgements & Thanks

With deepest thanks to my sister Margaret, Aileen George, Susan Conti, Julie Lawson, Julie Adam, Kate Ashton, Mairi Sutherland, and Jo Mulkerrin.

A special thank you to all the members of forWORDS, The Forres Writing Group (past and present) and John Glenday.

Previously publishing as Helen Addy, some of these poems, or earlier versions of them, have appeared in the following publications and anthologies:- *Gutter, Northwords Now, Happenstance's Blame Montezuma, Indigo Dreams' Heart Shoots, The Waterhouse Review, The Poet's Republic, Far Off Places, Southlight, and From Glasgow to Saturn.*

A Highlander at Glasgow Uni won 2nd Prize in the 2012 Highland Literary Salon poetry competition judged by John Glenday.

20 Primrose Street, 1972 was shortlisted in the Glasgow Women's Library/Dragon's PEN 'Moving' writing competition in 2012.

Myiasis was Runner-Up in the 2013 BBC Proms Poetry competition judged by Don Paterson and Ian McMillan.

Dust to Dust was Commended in the William Soutar Writing Prize, 2013.

The Bereaved One was Runner-Up in the National Galleries of Scotland Writing Competition, Adult Poetry, 2014.

Missing Space was Highly Commended in The Baker Prize, English Poetry, 2014.

Twitter @h_allison_poet

CONTENTS

For my daughters, Hannah and Holly,
and for Malcolm, husband of my heart

The Gooseberry Tree

*'It's alright, says Mose,
I shall wait till it grows,
hang me up on the gooseberry tree.'* – Folk song

On a cassette unwinding in a loft of warped boards,
my father's voice is scratched bark and strong branch,
the song rooted in darkness and wit (I take years to get it),
his baritone – a scaffold building itself downwards from leaf
to earth black and bricked, where death shuts out and seals in,
the background silence broken only by my mother closing
a door and going out, the last verse a tree standing small,
berries preserved in 1983, tart sweetness, soft fruit.

Quercus

This god threatened cars,
overhung tender houses,
his roots cracking the pavement.
Branded with a cross,
chainsaws cut through his limbs,
his bark falling like ash.

Denuded of life,
even the moon recoils,
but his black trunk is a totem,
the mouths of his white stumps
repeating the old myths,
his songs hung in the throats of birds.

Indecent Proposal

Moonlight, city centre building site,
my mother pissing in the rubble
as my father holds up her rented gown,
I've seen everything now, Rita,
we might as well get married,
concrete columns tree-ringed with laughter,
the streets of Glasgow running with gold.

The Snake

Great Aunt Lily turned day into night,
tried to buy bread at the pub in her slippers,
and gave all her jewellery to strangers.
My father searched for her serpent ring
in pawn shops, jewellers' windows,
and on the hands of silent neighbours.
Forty years on,
I pursue the snake I have never seen.
She is coiled around air or finger,
her tongue licking her golden tail.
Though her eyes have faded,
she will know my father's emerald gaze,
deep-set in the bezel of my face.

Aokigahara

From a path posted with helplines,
veins of coloured tape run ragged
to a clearing, now completely his,
new boots slipped from silent bones.

A yellow tent holds a suicide manual,
two days' water, half drunk.
His decision made whole by an even rope,
the beckoning finger of a strong branch.

His belt buckle bleeds rust into the earth,
blurred last words nailed to a trunk,
his photographs like sloughed skin,
still adrift in Mount Fuji's sea of trees.

Fragments

The cancer ward walls
white out his stories,
your fingerprints
on photographs
blur his features,
blacken his hair.
Memory dissects him,
his last legs limping
from toilet to bed,
one useless hand
held in the other.
Only his eyes
remain whole,
how they roamed your face
like a lighthouse beam,
even the spaces of dark
keeping you safe.

20 Primrose Street, 1972

Barely room for cigarette smoke,
my parents spent Sundays in bed.
Bicycles hung on nail-flecked walls,
three tables stacked in the kitchen,
their flat full to the gunnels
with furniture for a future house.

After a blonde first footer,
came two burglaries and dead twins,
treasures scattered across the city.
Flitting to a quiet town in Moray,
Glasgow shrank to a buttonhole,
raw edges softening as they made it through.

Cathay

Butting your wheel, head heavy
with tumours, a blind rabbit
stops your red bicycle. At twelve,
with neither weapon nor will,
you watch the wind stroke its fur,
the same hushed wind that
twenty five years on settles
what you never won,
scampering over the fields
like childhood, air tasted
and then sprung.

Rita Black

Pale survivor of scarlet fever and diphtheria,
her shoulders arched against the Glasgow sky,
dark chocolate sweetening her tongue.
Black Magic was her playground name.

Sixty years later, she gave her daughter a box.
Blind to its history, the girl left in untouched.
Under the cellophane, the red ribbon tightened,
soft centres hardened into bone.

Skelf

Cleaning abandoned,
you warn against infection,
our heads soft-focused through
dirty glass, lodged deep under
my nail, I carry it between rooms,
house to house, everywhere I go,
unlike us, I'm hoping it
doesn't work itself out.

The Bereaved One
After John Bellany's painting

The book of grief turns its own pages,
her hands hidden in a man's robe,
a yellow scarf like lightning,
the dark headboard housing
eyes long extinguished,
but her sleeves full of doves,
wild heather in their beaks,
a sea of blankets waiting
to be crossed.

The Ring

Heavy and mottled as a bruise, my mother's ring
isn't hers or mine, stolen in the Sixties from a lassie
washing her hands in the Barra's loos, its milky, polished eye
sits tight on my finger, fidget spinner for a dark past,
thieved knuckle duster, the stone's broken veins like
my mother's wind-burned face, it skews my handwriting,
catches on doors, history refusing to be left unattended.

Doorstep

Baby shoes, to heels and hob-nails,
I have lifted four generations
through the front door.

Scoured with hard-worn hands,
I roughen women's knees,
but am caressed by their skirts.

Husband and wife sit sharing
a cigarette, the entwined smoke
lengthening the last minute dark.

Imprinted with leavings,
the beginning of every journey,
I am a clear path, a stepping stone.

The Black Hole

Parents dying in June two years apart,
the month forms a black hole
in the centre of the calendar.
From the car behind,
the sun glints off my father's hearse,
each bend a small chance
to practise never seeing him again,
my mother patting my hand,
her rings sparking against mine.

At her cremation, the month repeated
its legacy of blue sky and empty heat,
every summer a burning season.
Years later, it's discovered that black holes spin,
swallowing gas and stars indiscriminately,
and the friction-heated matter falling in
become the brightest objects in space,
catalysts for the evolution of new galaxies.
I touch June's page, and wait for her pull.

On not Looking at Van Gogh's Almond Blossom in Red

Toasting the print's unopened tube with a glass of Merlot,
inside the mad flowers and floating limbs, blossom bursting
like secrets, petals notebook white, the crimson a meteor sky,
a mouth open with answers, but like all hope it must be returned,
pale branch on post office scales, the swept clean wall staying blue,
but the heart blood-rich, red traffic lights like haloes, the autumn walk
snowberries like beacons, each running, barking dog a signal to the body
to stand still, be safe, but the ear, the ear itself must roar.

Ardeonaig

for Julie Lawson

Finding a dead sheep in the burn,
no WiFi and death turns us giddy,
not YouTube, but ewe's tubes
doubling us over in the grass.
Stomach bloated like a pillow,
legs loosely crossed like
a sleeping woman's arms,
we crave a stick to move her,
but there are no trees, her wool
sodden with rain, her head
hard gone against the rocks.

Myiasis

The hedge you think is full of bees,
the hum sweetening your breakfast,
each garden flower living forever,
hides a rabbit corpse,
a thousand blow flies droning.
Burrowing in your ear like larvae,
their music fills each chamber,
the brain slowly muted,
then eaten away.

On the Road to Moniack Mhor

Car overheating in a passing place,
my parents pick stones from the road.
Dad's laughter is mediator to light
and dark mingling in his palm,
Mum scatters hers like seed,
sudden birds lifting from the hills.
The sun finding no argument,
leaves the conversation,
head bowed, circling on.

The Rainbow

Nebuliser whirring,
my father's beard jewelled
with saline drops, the man
in the next bed flailing his arms
again, hitting the switch,
both men choking on quiet air.
My father's good arm lifting a jug,
flinging water skywards, the glittering
arc shot through with colour,
the splash crowning the man's head,
blue and white nurses gathering,
my father's breath jagged
as lightning, one last strike
before the sky goes out.

Reader's Digest Trees and Shrubs of Britain
for Margaret

My mother's name and address handwritten inside,
she'd write *Stolen from Helen Allison* on school labels,
fear and guilt being branches of the same tree, a holly
to be exact, the hedge at the bottom of our road where
my runaway sister waited for the friend that did not come,
the hole we used as a shortcut to primary school, its crown
chopped off as we grew, but the book says it's unlucky
to cut it down, its long-lasting berries warding off spirits,
its white wood dense, hard and heavy; my mother's heart.

Woodend Hospital, MRI

It's the circular corridors, the large needle and slow limbs,
the creeping cold as the dye moves through your veins,
the fear claustrophobia could start right now, the poem
you learnt by heart moving your lips, the kindness
of cafe volunteers, the forty-five minute wait for the taxi
that arrives when you get the bus with no change,
the bright Tesco, dark car park underneath, the train
home passing the town where you know he lives,
not yet his name, the future a magnet with one pole,
every cell cancered or clean, surging towards it.

The Old Pieces

I see the *please help* sign before I recognise the man,
Davie from the auction mart, my Dad's pal,
cap still high on his head, the same dark denim
but his face skelped, blanket slipping off
his knees, his voice a drink-deepened Irish,
thanking folk who throw in their change.
I'm about to hand him a tenner, ask if he
remembers my Dad, the bidding, the treasures,
but his eyes are like tarnished mirrors,
and I remember the gilded, convex one
hung in the living room, my Dad neatening
his tie, the antique glass warping his features
into slight asymmetry, how I thought for years
he had one eyebrow slightly higher than the other,
disapproving, judgemental, but just the old pieces
playing their tricks on memory, Davie's eyes
like runes I can't decipher, can't disturb.

Great Granny was a Go-er

The only photograph of Mary Margaret Black,
she's posing in a Glasgow studio, one hand resting
on a fake picket fence, pinched cheeks and waist,
I'll change ma name and ma man as many times
as I please. Ma great-granddaughter can hae ma face,
I dinna need naething and naebody to lean on.

The Heart of the Poem

Striking the motorcyclist below the knee,
a barn owl explodes like a burst pillow,
the biker's boot filled with shit and feathers.

Braking hard beside the bridge,
he wipes the leather black,
breathes the air outside his helmet.

Lying outstretched on the road,
one wing covers the owl's heart,
a red purse emptying.

Bleeding miles into the forest,
the rider spends what remains,
wavering beauty, definite flight.

My Father's Forty Year Calendar

Though he fell thirty years short,
I swivel the year over the month,
red marking the years that leap.
Green marble holding metal
plates, the etched galleon doesn't
add up, the same way his tattoo
didn't, blurred blue beneath hair,
a thistle once, then an inkblot test
for every decade, my scores aiming
to please, missing the mark.

The Wrong Side of the Fence

Turn a corner and you lose the loch,
but the split tree holds water like a gourd,
a rusted pipe among the roots,
white lichen delicate as flowers,
cow hair spun through the bark,
the bracken so brown it's purple,
and the only shine a flue
on the last white house, the smoke
meeting you coming back,
each slip a fall into something else.

5 Castle Street

I'm night-running towards my childhood,
my father's gates lean from their hinges,
the paving stones bedded with weeds.
A red car curves onto the gravel drive,
I crouch on the pavement to retie laces,
wait for the man to unlock the door.
He turns the key while pulling the handle tight,
a family trick now performed by strangers.
The door opens and there's the light switch,
a body's width of wallpaper, then it shuts.
Hall patterned like branches poking through mist,
the switch a yellowed ornament refusing to fall.
Street lights give one last minute of dark,
before setting fire to the past.

The Beeches

for M.J.H

Even the broken-armed among them
touch their neighbours, the tunnel
not quite long enough but dark,
your lit eyes torching, mine
shuttering each grey torso,
kilts of branches soft against
the verges, taller side by side.

The Viewing

Smelling of chemicals
and fresh shirts,
his coffin is too big,
or he is too small,
his cheek an envelope
waiting for my lips
to fasten him down,
and send him away.
The assistant pats
his pocket, his glasses
tucked inside,
He looks good,
the intimacy, the lie.

Sugar Sisters

She's got skinny shifting sugar,
no been the same since her man
fell heid first into a boiling vat,
me wishing I'd no told him
to awa and bile it, the week afore.
Her sweeter than me, ma spade
heavier than her rake, the syrup
smell coats our hair like lacquer,
Greenock gales scooring the docks,
and Jamaica just the treacled,
dark street where we live.

The Cicada

Masquerading as a brown, plastic fly,
the Art Deco cicada, thorax of darkest red,
silver brooch like an insect collector's pin,
its hollow abdomen a sound box for a voice
of constant pitch, curved wings folded
as it drinks from willow, oak, cypress,
maple, its camouflaged eyes quiet
on earthen dresses, nocturnal song
softening at the nearness of you.

Summer's Last Glass of Wine

On the horizon the trees are doubling,
the cracks in the garden wall
closing like babies' fists.
My necklace is a silken trickle,
your lowering face like the sun
slipping from the sky.
The bottle dozes on the grass,
the breeze pouring a song into its mouth,
glasses chiming back the hours.

Dust to Dust

In the drawer of the chiffonier,
his overturned box of snuff,
its miniature dunes clogging
the innards of broken clocks.

Amplifying your childhood,
his coughing multiplied,
voice dry as tobacco,
cancer crumbling him to dust.

A pinch is all you need,
his ash chalking your hands,
your fists like stoppered urns,
each grasp the tightest, the last.

Scourie

for M.J.H

Wind sheening the rocks,
the bay's criss-crossing waves
make lancet windows full of sky,
a seal's head suspended like rain,
the jetty's red life belt like lipstick
on a saint, clouds reminding
mountains they can change,
the cemetery like dominoes
chapping, salt softened stone
keeping the loved.

Isle of Man, July 1955

Ears to rival Clark Gable,
a pretty girl on each knee,
neither my mother.

He insists the photograph was staged,
girls placed like empties on a bar,
but one laughs open-mouthed at his jokes,
the other leans into him, completely relaxed.

He is twenty one and ebullient as beer,
Dorothea Marshall is signed on the back,
he already knows her number.

When I Die,
Don't Make Me Into an Egg-Timer

Her eyes glassy, my mother's face
sand-shifts, sunken hours
slipping through her
fingers,
the world without her
hard-boiled, a shell without
a centre, a crack in everything.

Missing Space

Scotland from space hung
in the hall, its glass sea
a mirror for leaving.
The print long gone,
you stand faceless,
yellow walls
a wheat field with no sky,
the hook snagging
your shadow,
hanging you out to dry.

The Namesake

Before her mother emerged
from the anaesthetic,
her father registered the birth,
the printed name
swimming through morphine,
to open another wound.

Named after
his mother who
tetanus slammed shut,
the child was the buckle
on her father's belt,
a slow tightening.

After her parents' deaths,
the name forms a knot
no tongue can untie,
two bound syllables,
dark ribbons of erasure
and belonging.

Visitation

Littering the beach with their luggage,
my dead parents appear in my dream.
My father miscounts money into my hand,
crumpled notes lifting in the breeze.
My mother wears a dress she wouldn't wear,
pouring her complaints into a shell.

Their cases floating on the tide,
I push their van along the seafront,
letting go as the engine fires.
My mother posts a sweet into my father's mouth,
their waving arms framed in the wing mirror,
wheels grinding pebbles into dust.

A Highlander at Glasgow Uni

Don't smile at strangers on the underground,
avoid eye contact at all costs,
let the chippy owner's *right enough*,
float you back home on a polystyrene plate,
tell the mad woman on your terrace
to spit her abuse elsewhere,
don't skip lectures to watch
the River Kelvin coursing by,
philosophy slipping through your fingers,
say no to drugs, stay naturally fucked up,
when the drunk who calls you *angel*,
flashes you at 8am,
don't step off the kerb,
when ringing home insist on
speaking to your father,
and after cutting off all your hair,
for God's sake put on some lipstick.

Trimming the Leaves

Out slips a four leaf
clover, unsteady on his
stalk, covered with dust.

Uncut pages held him,
the knife granting sunshine
decades too late.

His luck now paper thin,
the garden a memory
that never came back.

A Father's Cure for Nightmares

Unbolt your head from the pillow
switch on the light
peel back the shadows
reclaim your white face
close your eyes
replay the nightmare
watch until the tape flickers
unravels across the sheets
crumple the film into a ball
hide it in a cupboard
fit me inside the lock like a key
pocket me where your childish
hands cannot reach me
where your grown fingers
pass through me like air

Strichen

In memoriam Roy Hutcheon 24.12.34 – 16.1.17

Your boyhood's snow drifted to the second floor
of number 93, your son reaching now to touch
the walls, his eyes lifted like yours under that visor,
but no brightness today, just the old high street,
its sash windows, the community park with dogs
and tea, the cemetery with your parents' grave,
your son's palm against it, his working hands turning
stone to uphold history, yours used to chisel young minds,
and both of you found here in February, a handshake
across the past, the white horse greying on the hill.

Washing My Hair in My Parents' Bathroom

"...poems are like dreams: in them you put
what you don't know you know." – Adrienne Rich

Foam crackling in my ears,
I pour water over my head,
clog the sink with a hundred strands,
and leave the towel how I wouldn't want to find it.

My dead father steps in,
tall and narrow like before I was born.
His black hair flickers under the light,
the mirror translates mine into straw.

The house from my childhood vanishes,
we walk along gleaming corridors,
pass chattering games rooms,
punctuated with healthy plants.

Leading me into a courtyard,
he points to a stone staircase,
his voice ending a decade of silence.
Go on, I'm right behind you.

Having Tea, 1956

Like an x-ray of his psyche, I hold
his photograph up to the light, his gaze
the same graced irritation I wear when
disturbed from reading, his book spread
open on his lap, his hair ruffled though
I thought he'd lost it in 1953, his cup
and saucer balanced on the arm of a chair
I've never seen, the background's blurred
bureau, the only solid strength in his bedroom,
while dying in 2002, this black and white,
clean-shaven, not yet my father's face,
how small his mouth was, how much
the beard I knew, concealed.

The Grandfather

Chime disabled the day you were born,
his tick assumed a father's rhythm,
face burnished like pride.
His weights shaped like pine cones,
cables rooted in sleek pulleys,
a door opened his walnut trunk,
the tenderest grain inside.

Under your grown fingers,
his brass pendulum wavered,
the key stumbled into its lock.
It was you who kept the heart
ticking inside his wooden body,
hands weary as death
working round the clock.

The Last Tree in Scotland

More Mel Gibson than William Wallace,
a dwarf Scots pine, an evergreen bastard,
deep roots and dense branches requiring
full sun, but taking what it can get,
its big brother the only large conifer
to return from the Ice Age, too tall now
to weather the storms of climate change,
the branch is passed to the wee man,
thriving in poor soil, slow to grow,
a flag of colour in the winter landscape.

The Mole

His nest of silver hair deserted,
unfastened buttons let him hover
in the dip of the throat.
His eyeless face
finds comfort in shadow,
but every swallow
brings him back to the light.
Lovers dig for him,
their lips filling his hollow bed
like pale worms mouthing
a blind particle of earth,
darkening with each bitter taste.

Doppelgänger

Cheating National Service, my father
moves to Jersey, the blurred biscuit-tinned
photos of St Helier, pub crawls and castles
telling nothing of his daily bus commute,
smiling strangers slapping him on the back,
offering him fags, his tie loosened as he plays
along, his doppelgänger's name the one he uses
when in trouble, the double I try and conjure
when I want him back, this one uncanny but
no cancer, tattoo-less and very much alive.

Last Light

With cancer she is a child again,
the drive to the hospital lit
by her pale face tilting at trees,
her voice proclaiming
everything clean and bright.
Her handbag lies open on her lap,
Turkish Delight spilling out,
whitening the seats.
The *darling* she gives to her daughter's name,
glistens like a wedding band, its yellow
piercing her final night like a star.
Her hands lie youthful against the sheets,
a fan scatters summer across her brow,
and the silence of the heart monitor
is a good husband's promise of sleep.